Understanding Genetics™

Classification of Living Organisms

Mark J. Lewis

ROSEN
PUBLISHING®

New York

My deepest appreciation goes to my wife, Jan, for her support, to my daughter, Nina, for her curiosity, and to Dr. Michelle Bowe, for teaching me the science of the classification of life.

Published in 2011 by The Rosen Publishing Group, Inc.
29 East 21st Street, New York, NY 10010

Library of Congress Cataloging-in-Publication Data

Lewis, Mark J.
Classification of living organisms / Mark J. Lewis. — 1st ed.
    p. cm. — (Understanding genetics)
Includes bibliographical references and index.
ISBN 978-1-4358-9535-5 (library binding)
1. Biology—Classification—Juvenile literature. I. Title.
QH83.L498 2011
570.1'2—dc22

                                       2009047624

Manufactured in the United States of America

CPSIA Compliance Information: Batch #S10YA: For further information, contact Rosen Publishing, New York, New York, at 1-800-237-9932.

On the cover: A display of butterflies shows various species that have been classified from tropical areas, including Florida, Kenya, Costa Rica, Thailand, and Malaysia.

Contents

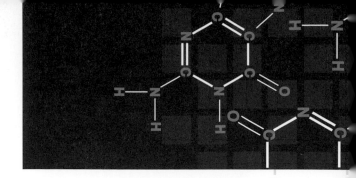

Introduction

Imagine you are in an electronics store. There are stereos, cell phones, televisions, and games. But this is an unusual store—a very messy store. All the items are scattered about randomly on shelves, on the floor, in closets, and in the storeroom. It is your job to organize items so people can find them easily. Just how would you arrange all these items? Would you arrange them by color? A store grouped by color would have all of the red cell phones grouped together with the red desk lamps and red laptop computers. But the rest of the cell phones would be in the next aisle with the black items or across the store with the silver items. This would not make shopping for cell phones easy. Perhaps color would not be a good method of classification. Size might work a bit better, but again, some televisions would be with the large stereos while others would be on the other side of the store with the cell phones. Why not just group all lamps together, all cell phones together, and all televisions together? Of course, that's what stores do: They group items by function—that is, by what they do.

Once the cell phones have been grouped together, there may still be more than one hundred different kinds of phones. So how should they be grouped? By model? By price? There are numerous ways to group items. Each has its advantages. Grouping living organisms is very similar. The advantage that store owners

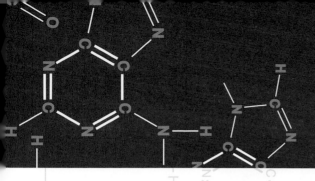

Stores display products according to their function so customers can easily find what they are looking for.

have is that items come with packages that describe their model, price, and functions. It is very different, though, when you first discover a new species of predator staring out at you, one with fangs bared, in the dim forest light.

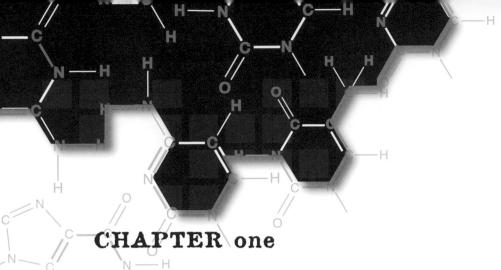

CHAPTER one

Early Classification

People have been trying to classify living organisms throughout history. People who used plants and animals as medicines were probably the first. Oral tradition suggests that, as early as 3000 BCE, Shen Nung, an emperor of China, supposedly tested hundreds of herbs for medicinal properties. Collected writings that have been credited to him describe 365 drugs and medical preparations made from living things and minerals. The Ebers Papyrus in Egypt, which dates to 1550 BCE, shows that plants were used as medicines. It uses a cursive form of hieroglyphics called hieratic script to name the plants and describe their properties.

The Earliest Rules

The first person to create a system of rules to classify living organisms was a Greek scientist and philosopher named Aristotle. He lived from 384 to 322 BCE. Aristotle pointed out that classification requires two steps. First, organisms have to be carefully described.

Imago hæc Aristotelis. Physicorum. *Libros scribentis, pertinet ad Libri.*

The Greek philosopher Aristotle (384–322 BCE) was the first person to propose rules for classifying organisms.

Think back to the electronics store. One way to classify items is by function. But before store owners can put an item in an aisle, they need to identify and describe the function of the item. Describing the function of a store item is easy because it comes in a package that specifies all that information. Describing a newly discovered species is not so simple. There is no label. The scientist must measure it and dissect it. He or she should also observe the new organism's behaviors and its habitat. Humans have been doing this for thousands of years.

Aristotle pointed out, however, that all those observations are not enough. Traits or features must also be carefully compared with the traits of similar organisms. Behavior, color, and habitat were features that were often used to classify animals. But some classifications are more complicated. Killer whales (orcas) and great white sharks, for example, both live in the ocean. They are both swimmers. Each animal also has a dorsal fin than helps keep the animal upright in the water. Both creatures are also predators, which means they hunt and kill other animals for food. Are they closely related? Actually, no. Aristotle

Great white sharks breathe by taking in water and passing it over their gills. Their constant motion, way of swimming with their mouths open, and their method of breathing is called ram ventilation.

pointed out that only some characteristics were appropriate for use in classification.

Consider the following: Many kinds of animals have two eyes. Lots of aquatic animals, which are animals that live in water, have fins. Many different kinds of animals are predators. These traits are not reliable for classification purposes. Aristotle worked to find more reliable traits to categorize living organisms. Does the animal lay eggs, like birds, fish, and reptiles? Or does the animal give birth to live young, like mammals? Is the animal cold-blooded, as reptiles and fish are or warm-blooded like mammals and birds? Does the animal breathe using gills or lungs? These traits proved to be far more reliable for classification. Consider the great white shark and killer whale. The great white shark produces eggs, which it holds inside its body, while the killer whale gives birth to a well-developed baby whale. The great white has a body temperature that is the same as the ocean around it. The killer

whale maintains a steady body temperature of about 98 degrees Fahrenheit (37 degrees Celsius). It has blubber to insulate itself from the cold ocean water. The great white shark breathes using gill slits. The shark's forward movement forces water into its mouth, then through the throat, and out through the gill slits. The shark uses its gill slits to extract oxygen from water flowing across its gills, so it

Killer whales come to the surface to breathe air into their lungs.

never needs to surface as long as the shark keeps moving. The killer whale uses lungs to breathe, just as humans do. It must surface to take giant breaths. It can then hold its breath for as long as fifteen minutes! Using Aristotle's early system, it becomes clear that although

This 1579 print depicts the Scala Naturae, or the Ladder of Nature, a principle about the line of perfection. Also called the Great Chain of Being, the diagram shows the classical idea of order in the universe with the lowest at the bottom and rising to the most perfect.

both whales and sharks swim, and have similar color and shapes, they are not as closely related as whales and people are—even though humans don't live in the water.

Naming new organisms was a major problem throughout the history of classification. People had been describing living organisms for thousands of years, but there was no common system of naming them. Often, they were just given names that described where they were found, like "flower of the river." The same organism might have twenty different names, which led to confusion. Aristotle put similar animals into groups called genera (plural for genus). It was a general category for any creatures Aristotle saw as being similar. Then he further divided the genera into different species.

Aristotle's System of Classification

Aristotle did try to put living and nonliving things in order. He saw living things in order from lowest to highest. Because Aristotle saw the universe as perfect, the chain was perfect. Each organism supposedly sat just below another more complex organism in perfect order with simple plants at the bottom and humans at the top. Aristotle also saw the universe as unchanging. Species did not change.

This idea of a chain organized from simple to complex was not a problem for classifying some creatures. A human is higher on the chain than a flea. It was, however, very difficult to explain exactly what "higher on the chain" meant. Did it mean "more intelligent than"? Or "more powerful than"? Or "morally superior to"? And what is superior—an oak or a maple? A dog or a cat? Aristotle had a hard time coming up with a set of rules to solve this problem. The other problem with this model was that it was not evolutionary. Aristotle saw life on Earth to be unchanging. His idea was, however, very important because it was perhaps the first attempt to put living organisms in order.

A Classification Misstep

One of Aristotle's early classification errors was his attempt to classify animals by how they moved. He saw three distinct groups: animals that fly, animals that swim, and animals that walk. Birds fly, fish swim, and humans walk. The main problem with this system quickly becomes apparent when one considers ducks. Many types of ducks spend most of their lives swimming. But they are not fish. These feathered, egg-laying creatures are clearly related to hawks, which rarely swim, and ostriches, which cannot fly. Are there any other problems in using this method? How about in the case of an alligator? This creature has scales like fish and lives much of its life in the water. But it breathes air and lays eggs, as a bird does. No fish has lungs. The alligator can live out of the water unlike fish. This system of using movement as a characteristic for classification was not successful in categorizing life on Earth.

An alligator is an example of an animal that did not fit well into Aristotle's classification system. Alligators can walk on land, but they are also powerful swimmers.

The earliest classifiers of life brought some order to the thousands of living things around them for two reasons. People tested plant and animal substances because of their medical needs. The scientist and philosopher Aristotle was very curious and simply wanted to figure out how things were related. Aristotle's contributions were particularly important because he created the basis for a standard system of naming and because he showed that the classification of living things requires two steps: the thorough description of each organism and the thoughtful comparison of similar organisms. He was also the first to try to put all living organisms in order. Though not all of his ideas were factually correct, they have influenced the way people look at living things for more than two thousand years.

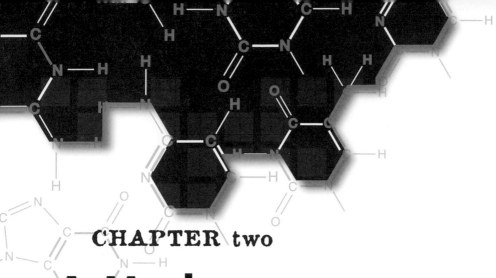

CHAPTER two

A Modern System Is Born

After Aristotle and his students died, much of his classification work was forgotten in the West. A great deal of it was lost or accidentally destroyed. In the ninth and tenth centuries, however, Arab scholars translated the writings of Artistotle and studied them. Through these scholars' writings, the works of Aristotle were reintroduced to people in the West. Because of Arab scholarship, Aristotle's work became the foundation of medieval philosophy, theology, and natural science.

Early Taxonomy

In the late 1500s, there was a renewed interest in describing the natural world. Unlike today, Renaissance scholars were often experts in many different fields of research. Many doctors were also botanists because plants were often used to treat illnesses. Andrea Cesalpino (1519–1603) was a doctor and botanist living in Italy during the sixteenth century. Cesalpino studied Aristotle's approach to classifying organisms. He used Aristotle's work to come up with his own

This statue of Italian doctor and botanist Andrea Cesalpino is in Florence, Italy. Cesalpino is often called the first taxonomist because he classified plants in a careful and logical manner.

classification method. Cesalpino is often called the first taxonomist because he used a logical approach to classification. Cesalpino carefully analyzed and compared all the plants he knew before selecting the characteristics he used to divide them into groups. Cesalpino classified more than 1,500 plants in his publications. He decided that seeds and seedlings were important characteristics to consider when dividing plant groups.

Two Swiss brothers, Gaspard and Jean Bauhin, followed up on Cesalpino's work. In 1623, Gaspard published *Pinax theatri botanici* (Illustrated Exposition of Plants), a book that listed more than six thousand species of plants. He grouped plants by genus and tried to keep the species names as short as possible. The book also helped clear up some of the confusion caused by repeated naming of plants.

One of the most significant scientists working on classification at that time was John Ray, an English scholar and naturalist who lived from 1627 to 1705. Ray was an ordained Anglican priest and he sought to uncover "God's natural order" by classifying organisms.

Ray looked at the idea of species differently from that of most scientists of his era. Most botanists focused on one or two character- istics when classifying plants. Ray looked at the total morphology, or the form and structure of the whole plant. He influenced other botanists to start looking at the total morphology of plants. Ray also noticed that plants could seemingly be neatly divided into two large groups based on their number of cotyledons. Cotyledons are leaflike parts of the embryo that serve as storage organs for nutrients. If a plant's seed contained one cotyledon, Ray called that plant a mono- cot. If a plant's seed contained two cotyledons, Ray called that plant a dicot. While monocots and dicots are still recognized as sub- classes of plants in some more recent classification systems, the dicots are no longer recognized in systems based on evolutionary relationships.

Besides his extensive work with plants, Ray also was one of the first scientists to promote the idea of fossils as forms of dead

LINNÆUS

Carolus Linnaeus simplified classification by shortening the name for organisms to two words. Linnaeus also recognized that small groups of organisms fit into larger hierarchical groups.

organisms. He did not, however, believe that God would let living things go extinct. Instead, Ray considered fossils of extinct organisms to be animals or plants that had not yet been discovered. He simply thought that they lived in some other part of the world. Toward the end of his life, Ray began to ask more questions about fossils and to wonder if Earth was actually older than traditional theology taught.

A New Taxonomist

In this flurry of work by numerous scientists with widely varying systems of classification, the work of one Swedish botanist stands out. Carolus Linnaeus (also known as Carl von Linné) was born in 1707. Like many noted taxonomists of his time, Linnaeus spent his childhood fascinated with plants. His father taught him the names of all the plants in their garden. When Linnaeus went to school, he often skipped class to look for plants in the countryside. Linnaeus's classmates nicknamed him "little botanist."

Linnaeus's parents wanted him to become a priest. However, Linnaeus showed little interest or talent for the subjects studied by priests. There was a doctor who taught at Linnaeus's high school who was impressed by Linnaeus's knowledge of plants. He convinced Linnaeus's father that Linnaeus should study medicine so he would be able to use his knowledge of plants in his career.

Linnaeus became a doctor and respected naturalist. He studied plants, animals, and minerals. He also thought a lot about how to best classify organisms. The problem with classification at Linnaeus's time was there were far too many systems of organization. People often gave plants long Latin names that described the plant. One name could have been "the red flower that grows by water." Linnaeus saw this as confusing and cumbersome. He did two things to help clarify this.

Sugar maples (Acer saccharum) and sycamore maples (Acer pseudoplatanus) both have characteristic maple leaves that have sharp points.

Binomial Nomenclature

Linnaeus reduced his names for organisms to one name with two parts. In 1753, Linnaeus published a plant book that introduced his binomial nomenclature method of naming organisms. He was not the first person to give organisms two-part names, but he was the first to consistently use such a system. Linnaeus applied some of the genus names created by the Bauhin brothers for the first name that is used to describe a whole group of similar organisms. The second name in Linnaeus's system was a one word species name. Sometimes Linnaeus took a word from descriptive names that other people had already given to the plant. Sometimes he made up his own. Linnaeus was the first person to use species names that did not always describe the plant. He sometimes named plants after people he knew. For example, a friend and fellow botanist, Elias Tillandz, disliked traveling by boat. Linnaeus named a genus of plants that does not grow well in damp soil *Tillandsia*, after his friend. He also named a small weed *Siegesbeckia* after his rival and critic, botanist Johann Siegesbeck.

Many species named during Linnaeus's time still have the same name today. Scientists still use Linnaeus's binominal system to give newly discovered species a name. The genus name, together with the species name for an organism, is called its scientific name. As in Linnaeus's time, scientific names for new species are still created using Latin or Greek words. Latin is more commonly used than Greek, so the scientific name for an organism is sometimes referred to as its Latin name. Scientific names are always italicized. The species name often describes a notable characteristic of the organism. For example, all maple trees belong to the genus *Acer*. *Acer* means "hard" or "sharp" in Latin, and it refers to the sharp points on the leaves of most maples. The scientific name for sugar maples is *Acer saccharum*. The sweet sap of sugar maples is used to make maple syrup. *Saccharum* means "sugar" or "sweet" in Latin.

Hierarchical Classification

In addition to his binomial naming system, Linnaeus also introduced a hierarchical system of organization. A hierarchy is an arrangement that divides large groups into smaller groups. The small groups can be placed in order beneath the title of the big group. For example, a high school has a hierarchical order. All students at the school are high school students. Within that large group of students, the students can be divided into seniors, juniors, sophomores, and freshmen. They can then be further divided into homerooms. But just like Linnaeus's system, the smaller groups have to fit neatly into the larger groups for the hierarchy to make sense. One organism or student cannot fit into more than one of the larger groups. For example, sports teams would not be a good group to include in a hierarchical diagram of a high school because team members would not all be in the same year of high school and not all students would be on a sports team. Linnaeus's system was a neat hierarchical system.

When Linnaeus was in his late twenties, he published his system for classifying animals and plants in a book called *Systema Naturae* (The System of Nature). The original edition of *Systema Naturae* was simply an eleven page list of all discovered plants and animals Linnaeus knew of, classified according to his hierarchical order. His hierarchical order differed from other work done previously. Throughout the years, Linnaeus added to his book, which, in its tenth edition in 1758, became a huge two-volume publication.

From Aristotle's time, organisms had been grouped with similar organisms in small groups on the genus level and then into the two very large kingdoms of plants and animals. Linnaeus created more levels in between. He created seven rankings in his hierarchy. Linnaeus's hierarchical ranking started with the very large kingdoms and went down through phyla (plural for phylum), classes, orders, families, genera (plural for genus) to the smallest unit of classification, species. *System Naturae* was the first classification

Grizzly bear	Black bear	Giant panda	Red fox	Abert squirrel	Coral snake	Sea star

KINGDOM Animalia

PHYLUM Chordata

CLASS Mammalia

ORDER Carnivora

FAMILY Ursidae

GENUS *Ursus*

SPECIES *Ursus arctos*

This chart shows the hierarchical classification of a grizzly bear into Linnaeus's seven groups. Grizzlies share some characteristics with all animals. They are most similar to black bears, with whom they share a genus.

scheme to group humans with monkeys as primates in the order Primata. Linnaeus's colleagues recognized he had a talent for putting things in order. Unlike Aristotle, Linnaeus did not often run into the problem of finding an organism that fit into more than one of his big categories.

Over his career, Linnaeus continued to add new species and findings to his *Systema Naturae*. Twelve editions of the book were published before he died. Linnaeus once remarked to a friend that he was upset about all the work he was putting into it. He, like many scientists of his time, simply thought that most living creatures had already been discovered and named! Even today, however, it is widely believed that only a small fraction of the actual living creatures on Earth have even been discovered.

Linnaeus's hierarchical system allowed taxonomists of the time to group living organisms based on increasing morphological similarity. Classification systems kept Linnaeus's hierarchy but ignored his classification of plants

	Red oak	Emperor penguin	Monarch butterfly
Kingdom	Plantae	Animalia	Animalia
Phylum	Tracheophyta	Chordata	Arthropoda
Class	Magnoliopsida	Aves	Insecta
Order	Fagales	Sphenisciformes	Lepidoptera
Family	Fagaceae	Spheniscidae	Nymphalidae
Genus	*Quercus*	*Aptenodytes*	*Danaus*
Species	*Quercus rubra*	*Aptenodytes forsteri*	*Danaus plexippus*

by flowers. Plant taxonomists preferred John Ray's use of total plant morphology.

With the hierarchical nature of Linnaeus' classification it became common to use another tool of classification called the dichotomous key. "Dichotomous" means divided into two parts. A tool that has been long used to organize things, the dichotomous key is simply a series of questions that, based on the answer, separates things into two groups.

One example is plant identification. Imagine a dendrologist, a tree scientist, is hiking through a remote forest on the western side of the Rocky Mountains in Oregon. She comes upon an unfamiliar tree and wonders if she is the first to discover it. Her dichotomous tree key asks a series of questions about the tree. Each question has only two possible answers. The first question asks, "Is the tree growing in the eastern or the western part of the United States?" She selects western and is directed to the second half of the book, where western trees are described. There she is asked, "Are the leaves broad or slender?" She sees that the leaves are slender and is directed to turn to page 305. She is then asked, "Are the leaves long, like needles, or short and stubby, like scales?" The leaves are quite short—many of them would fit on the tip of her finger. She chooses short leaves and the guide directs her to page 322. She is asked, "Are the leaves arranged side by side, so the branch is flat or are the leaves arranged in a corkscrew pattern around the branch?" She sees that the branch is quite flat. The dichotomous key directs her to turn to page 330 where there is a list of six trees growing west of the Rockies that have slender, stubby leaves that grow flat from the branch.

Morphology, Embryology, and Other Methods of Taxonomy

Today, scientists do not always use morphology to classify organisms. But, morphological similarities can still be used to explain how

Scientists use the color patterns on monarch butterflies and emperor penguins to help classify them.

some organisms are classified. For example, it is easy to see that a northern red oak tree and an emperor penguin are both living organisms. They both grow, change, and reproduce. It is also easy to see that northern red oaks and emperor penguins belong to different kingdoms. The northern red oak is a plant. Plants belong to the kingdom Plantae. A penguin is an animal, so it belongs in the kingdom Animalia.

A monarch butterfly is an animal, too. Penguins and butterflies both have wings but are very different animals. Look at the chart on page 25 to see how the classification of emperor penguins and monarch butterflies differ.

An emperor penguin is in the phylum Chordata. All animals in this phylum have three particular structures at some point in their life cycle: a notochord, a hollow dorsal nerve, and pharyngeal slits. A monarch butterfly has a segmented body and jointed appendages, so it belongs to the phylum Arthropoda.

An emperor penguin has feathers. Like all birds, the emperor penguin belongs to the class of animals with feathers, called Aves. Monarch butterflies have antennae and six pairs of legs so they belong in the Insecta class.

Penguins are funny-looking water birds that stand upright. All penguins belong to the order Sphenisciformes and the family Spheniscidae. All butterflies have a long tube, called a proboscis, that they use to suck nectar. All butterflies belong to the order Lepidoptera. All butterflies that have short front legs that they can't use for walking belong to the Nymphalidae family.

Emperor penguins share the genus *Aptenodytes* with king penguins. Emperor and king penguins are larger and somewhat more colorful than other penguins. All butterflies in the *Danaus* genus have orange wings with black veins and white-spotted black margins.

Emperor penguins are taller than king penguins and have a distinct yellow pattern near their ears. One can distinguish a

The platypus and the duck both live near water and have bills. But a platypus is a mammal and a duck is a bird. The bill is a homoplastic trait that they each inherited from different ancient ancestors.

monarch from other similar-looking *Danaus* butterflies by measuring its wings. Monarch butterflies have a wingspan of about 3 to 5 inches (7.6 to 12.7 centimeters).

Linnaeus and many scientists of his time classified organisms solely based on physical characteristics or morphology. Since Linnaeus, scientists have discovered additional useful tools for looking for relationships between organisms. Some scientists compare how different animals develop before they are born. The science of embryology has revealed relationships that were not obvious just from looking at physical characteristics of animals. For example, the blue whale, which is a mammal, and the rattlesnake, which is a reptile, both have similar protective sacs that surround their embryos. The crocodile and the bald eagle both lay eggs with thick shells. Each case suggests that the organisms share a common ancestor.

Remember that taxonomists have always looked for homologous characters. Homologous characters are traits that two different species share because they have a common ancestor. For example, humans and bats both have five digits at the end of their forelimbs. These digits form fingers in humans. In bats, the five digits form their wing bones. This is called homology. Deciding which homologous characters can be used to separate different groups and show relationships can be tricky.

Sometimes two species will appear similar even though they are not closely related. They may have similar characters simply because they independently adapted to similar environments. The duck-billed platypus is a strange animal. Platypuses lay eggs like birds and reptiles. As its name suggests, the duck-billed platypus has a bill that resembles a duck bill. Platypuses also have hair, and mothers produce milk to feed their babies. Biologists have decided that platypuses are mammals. They inherited their hair and mother's milk traits from a common ancestor they share with other mammals. The duck's bill and the platypus's bill are called a homoplastic trait. Homoplastic means similar in structure but not in origin. Homoplastic

Scientists named this Venezuelan diving beetle Agaporomorphus colberti *to honor the comedian Stephen Colbert.*

characters tend to evolve on organisms that live in similar environments. Ducks and platypuses both live near water and find their food in the water. Both animals likely evolved bills because they are useful for catching and eating small food items found in the water. The duck and platypus, however, inherited their bills from unrelated ancestors.

Modern Species Naming

Like Linnaeus, today's scientists are still discovering and renaming species. In 2009, scientists named a diving beetle they discovered in Venezuela after the comedian Stephen Colbert. The beetle's scientific name is *Agaporomorphus colberti*.

In 2005, the genus of *Acacia* trees and shrubs was split into three different genera by botanists. Australian botanists waged a campaign to allow the Australian species to keep the name *Acacia*. *Acacia* species make up a large percentage of wild and commercially grown plant species in Australia. The botanists successfully argued that changing the scientific names of the almost one thousand *Acacia* species in Australia would confuse people, hurt the horticulture industry, and require many plant publications to be rewritten. Australian *Acacia* trees, such as *Acacia decora*, were allowed to keep their names. African, Asian, and American acacias now have the new generic names *Vachellia* and *Senegalia*.

When a new species is discovered or an old species is renamed, the name for the new species must meet the requirements of an international organization. If it is a plant, the name is approved by the International Committee on Systematics of Prokaryotes. New animal species names are approved by the International Commission on Zoological Nomenclature. New bacterial species are approved by the International Code of Nomenclature of Bacteria.

The requirements for naming species differ from organization to organization but the major requirements are the same. It is important, of course, not to repeat names that have already been used. It is also important that just like the kingdom, the phylum, the class, the order, and the family, both the genus and species are written in Latin. People of all nations and languages use scientific names, and Latin is currently a language that no nation calls its own, so it is seen as a neutral language.

The species name must also follow the binomial naming system that has been used now for hundreds of years. Each name must have a genus and a specific epithet, or specific name. The genus is capitalized while the specific epithet is not. Both parts of the name must be italicized. One example is the scientific name of humans: *Homo sapiens*. The genus is *Homo*. The specific name is *sapiens*. The two parts together are the species name.

The ranks of Linnaeus's system are one useful method of organizing living things. Except for the rank of species, however, they are arbitrary. That means they have no particular value. There is no definition for the terms "families" or "classes" except to say that one is bigger than another. For example, families fit within a class. Though Linnaeus's contributions would remain important, other methods of classifying living things would soon arise.

CHAPTER three

Evolutionary Relationships: The Dawn of Phylogenetics

The best-known scientist who tried to organize the world's creatures is Charles Darwin. Darwin lived from 1809 to 1882. His work is still debated and discussed today.

Darwin's Early Work

As a child, Darwin lived in the English countryside. Young Darwin was interested in nature and science. In his late teens, Darwin studied medicine. But, unlike many other famous taxonomists before him, Darwin did not become a doctor. Despite Darwin's curiosity about the natural world and his enjoyment of plant and animal studies, medical procedures made him queasy. Darwin quit medical school after two years of study.

After Darwin dropped out of medical school, Darwin's father decided that Darwin should be a clergyman. Darwin returned to the university to finish a degree. Again, he was drawn to natural history.

He took courses on religion but also took more courses in botany and zoology. When Darwin was not studying, he would often spend his free time collecting beetles.

After Darwin finished his university degree, a friend and botany professor, John Stevens Henslow, recommended that Darwin go on an upcoming ocean voyage with Captain Robert Fitzroy. Captain Fitzroy was looking for a naturalist to collect and describe plants and animals on an exploration trip to South America for the British Royal Navy.

The HMS *Beagle* set sail from England in December 1831. The voyagers returned to England almost five years later. During the trip, Darwin wrote detailed notes and drew sketches of the organisms he encountered on his journey. He also collected numerous plant, animal, and mineral specimens. Years later, Darwin used his observations from his *Beagle* journey to come up with his theory of evolution by natural selection.

Evolution and Natural Selection

Darwin is often called the Father of Evolution. In truth, Darwin was not the first person to suggest that different species descended from common ancestors. Darwin and another scientist, Alfred Russel Wallace, working independently, each made the major step of explaining what caused evolution. Both Darwin and Wallace pointed out that the organisms best adapted to their surroundings would survive and pass on their traits to their offspring. Darwin called this mechanism natural selection, which became known as "survival of the fittest." Darwin's name became forever attached to these ideas shortly thereafter when he published his theory of evolution by natural selection in 1859 in his hugely influential book *On the Origin of Species*.

A species is a group of organisms that is able to breed together to produce offspring that also live and reproduce. The whole group

A nineteenth-century watercolor by artist Conrad Martens shows the HMS Beagle in Murray Narrows, along the coast of South America. Charles Darwin observed and described many plants and animals on his nearly five-year voyage on the Beagle.

doesn't have to live in the same place. On the *Beagle* trip, Darwin noticed that many similar species were slightly different from one another. He surmised that their differences helped them succeed in their own habitats. For example, on the remote Galapagos Islands, he noticed various species of finches had differently shaped beaks. These islands were far too distant for much finch migration from the mainland. In addition, the various islands were quite far apart from each other. In fact, Darwin suspected that the finches on each island probably stayed on that island permanently.

One major difference between the islands was the types of food available to the finches. On one island, the finches ate insects and had narrow, sharp beaks. On another island, where the finches ate more larvae and buds, the finches' beaks were broad and hooked. There turned out to be thirteen individual species of finches. Each had a slightly differently shaped beak that was best suited for getting at the food most available. Darwin hypothesized that long ago, a single type of finch came to live on all the islands. Perhaps, he said, they were blown from the mainland while flying through a storm. Over many generations, the finches best equipped for each island survived to pass on their traits to their offspring.

While living in England, Darwin noticed that domesticated pigeons could be bred to have certain traits. Darwin used his finch, pigeon, and other observations to come up with an idea of how species arose from common ancestors.

Darwin's process of natural selection has several steps. First, Darwin proposed that offspring with advantageous traits, such as beaks better suited for eating the available seeds, will survive better than other offspring without these traits. Offspring that survive will produce their own offspring. Those offspring will inherit the beneficial traits from

1. Geospiza magnirost
3. Geospiza parvula.

2. Geospiza fortis.
4. Certhidea olivasea.

These sketches show the beaks of two finch species that Darwin observed on the Galapagos Islands. Often called "Darwin's finches," they include the ground finch (1), the medium ground finch (2), the small tree finch (3), and the warbler finch (4).

their successful parents. Different environments lead to different advantageous traits becoming prominent in offspring. Over time, organisms living in diverse environments become distinct enough to develop into different species—they lose the ability to interbreed.

Classification by Phylogenetics

Darwin described species as branches of a tree. Branches were formed when one common ancestor changed over time into many different species. This idea of new species branching off from common ancestors was new in Darwin's time. Now it is an accepted field of study called phylogenetics.

Phylogenetics is the study of evolutionary relationships between organisms. Before Darwin, systematic scientists looked for homologous traits to help classify organisms into groups. However, they simply thought of the homologous traits as important consistent traits, not as traits that were inherited from common ancestors. Once scientists began using evolutionary relationships, classification made more sense. Relationships between organisms could be sketched out in phylogenetic trees.

A phylogenetic tree is similar to a family tree. Family trees have branches that show relationships between individuals in a family. In a family tree, it is easy to see who are the parents of one individual and to see other ancestors, such as great-grandparents. Phylogenetic trees show groups, instead of individuals. One parent or common ancestral group usually branches off into two different groups.

When scientists correctly classify an organism, they try to find its true place in the phylogenetic tree. Correctly classifying organisms can be a difficult task. The task is easier now, however, than it was before Darwin's theory of evolution by natural selection. Before Darwin, scientists had trouble explaining the developmental ideas that later became known as divergence and convergence. Divergence is the splitting of one species into others. When one species becomes separated into different environments, the groups in unalike environments adapt to become distinct species over time. After Darwin, scientists were able to link differences in similar species to differences in their environments.

Before the theory of evolution by natural selection was accepted, scientists didn't understand how or why distantly related species inherit traits that appear similar. Scientists now know that the similar traits are from different ancestors and have evolved separately; they call this convergence, or parallel evolution. The similar species may look alike but they are not closely related. They look alike in some ways because they exist in like environments. In those environments, it is an advantage to have particular traits. Similar traits formed by convergence are known as homoplasies.

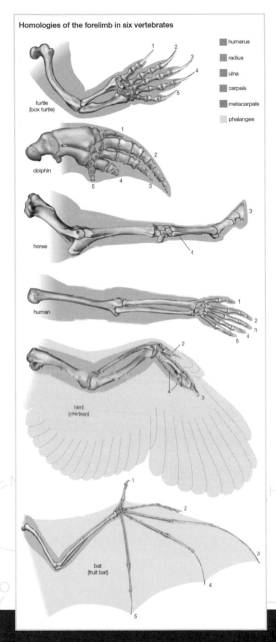

Homologies of the forelimb in six vertebrates

humerus
radius
ulna
carpals
metacarpals
phalanges

turtle (box turtle)

dolphin

horse

human

bird (chicken)

bat (fruit bat)

Turtles, dolphins, horses, humans, birds, and bats are all vertebrates that share a common ancient ancestor. Their forelimbs have evolved over time to take different forms.

An Example of Convergence and Parallelism

At first look, whale sharks (Rhincodon typus) and North Atlantic right whales (Eubalaena glacialis) might appear to be closely related. They both are large ocean animals that have large blunt heads with big mouths. They have similar coloration: dark gray or brown on the top of their bodies and lighter underneath.

Whale sharks and right whales are both filter feeders with similar diets. Whale sharks feed by opening their large mouths and sucking in water. Plankton, small fish, small invertebrates, and fish eggs in the water get stuck on the whale shark's gill rakers. Gill rakers are bristles that catch small creatures in the water before the water enters the whale shark's gills. The plankton and other creatures are passed on to the whale shark's stomach.

Right whales have baleen plates inside their mouths. The baleen plates are similar to the whale shark's gill rakers. They look like fringes. But the right whale has baleen plates instead of teeth. The whale shark has gill rakers and teeth. Right whales feed on plankton that gets stuck on their baleen plates.

Though whale sharks live in the warm waters of the world and right whales in the colder waters, the ranges of the two species overlap slightly in waters near the Florida coast. Whale sharks and right whales look and act alike because they have adapted to feeding on similar prey in similar environments. But, they come from very different

lineages. Like other sharks, whale sharks belong to the class Chondrichthyes. Chondrichthyes are cartilaginous fish. Their skeletons are made of cartilage (similar to that on the tip of the human nose).

Whale sharks are often called the largest fish in the ocean. Fish are not a recognized group in taxonomic classification. But when people talk about fish, they usually mean the aquatic animals with skeletons, gills, and fins. Scientists also know that fish are not mammals. By this definition, whale sharks are the largest fish in the ocean. They can grow up to 40 feet (12.2 meters) or more.

Right whales are bigger than whale sharks. They grow up to 50 feet (15.24 m) or more. Right whales belong to the class Mammalia and the order Cetacea. Cetacea includes all whales, dolphins, and porpoises. Cetaceans are more closely related to cows than to whale sharks.

The observation that whale sharks and right whales have similar features that were passed on from adaptations of different ancestors is a good example of convergence and parallolism. The large size of whale sharks and right whales is useful to both species because few ocean predators will attack huge animals. Plankton is plentiful in most parts of the ocean, so their diet is also suitable for a large animal. Both species come from ancestors that adapted over time to use a sievelike system to get their food.

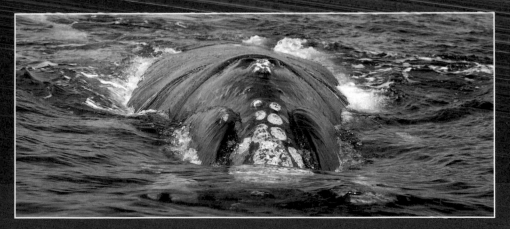

A whale shark (left) and right whale (right) are not closely related species. The two species, however, evolved similar traits, a process called convergence.

The Use of Traits in Phylogenetics

Some traits change quickly in species. Others do not. The traits that change quickly are often ones where different forms are beneficial in different environments. For example, all mammals are believed to have descended from an ancestor with five toes or digits. Some mammals such as primates still have five digits on their feet but many, such as horses, do not. Different species of mammals have feet that come in different shapes and textures. Foot shape, texture, and the number of digits are characteristics that vary in relation to

Biologists believe that all mammals descended from an ancestor who had five digits. The digits on each limb of a horse, such as this Shetland pony, evolved to become one weight-bearing digit.

what is best for how and where a particular mammal species lives and moves.

All mammals have hair. Beavers have dense fur. Dolphins are born with a tiny amount of whiskerlike hair on their chin that they lose as they grow. But all mammals have hair made of a protein called keratin while modern reptiles, amphibians, fish, and birds do not. This hair on mammals is called a conserved characteristic because it appears on all mammals. Hair on other creatures, such as hairy caterpillars, is not made of keratin. Conserved characteristics do not disappear quickly as species evolve. The fact that these traits

Hair is a conserved characteristic in mammals. A chimpanzee's hair has a different amount of keratin from that of a human's, and its hair stops growing at a certain length.

last a long time makes these characteristics useful for classifying related organisms.

As science advanced after Darwin, scientists discovered that many organisms that were classified in the same groups for morphological reasons also shared common traits that could not be seen. For example, plants in the same family may produce similar chemical substances. Some but not all members of the Solanaceae (nightshade family) produce nicotine. Closely related species also share particular DNA sequences. More ways to analyze species can make it easier to see how different species are related. New information can also change ideas about classifications. Many classifications of organisms are still being changed or decided based on new evidence from chemical and DNA analysis.

46

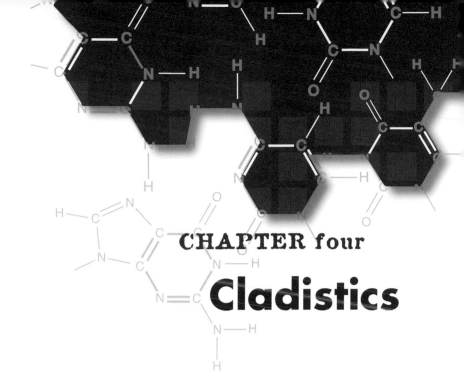

CHAPTER four
Cladistics

For a while, scientists continued to struggle to classify living organisms using the evolutionary relationships each organism had to other organisms, known as phylogenetics. One way to discover how and where different species branch off from one another in phylogenetic trees is to use a process called cladistic analysis, or cladistics.

How Cladistics Works

A clade is a group made of an ancestor and all of its descendants. The Greek word *clados* means "branch." Cladists, people who use cladistics, look for branching relationships within a selected group of species using shared traits. Some examples of characters that are analyzed are tooth length, beak shape, and brain size. The cladist uses the branching relationships to make logical assumptions about which characters a common ancestor had. The common ancestor's form of the character is called a conservative trait or a plesiomorphy. The changed form of a character that some newer ancestors have adapted to is called a derived trait or an apomorphy. The branched

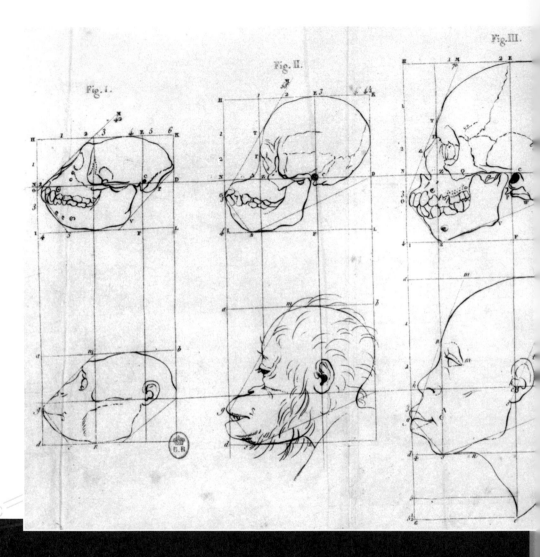

This illustration that was published in the late 1700s depicts shared conservative traits in ape and human skulls.

diagram created by cladistic analysis of a group of species is called a cladogram.

Cladistic analysis can use physical, molecular, or even behavioral characters. Today, DNA or RNA base sequences are often used

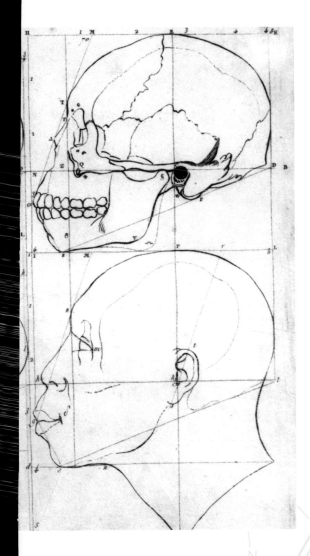

in cladistics. When scientists use DNA to construct a cladogram the shared characters they use are small sections of DNA. They look for sections of the gene code that remain stable and others that change in related organisms. The organisms with the most sections that are the same are often thought to be most closely related.

Cladistics also assumes a clade divides into two new lineages when it branches. Apparent multiple splits simply indicate a need for further study to reduce all divisions into two-way splits. Cladograms show the branching split off of two lineages at nodes. Cladistic analysis sounds relatively simple, but like all classification techniques, establishing correct relationships between species can be difficult. For example, one species may share an apomorphy with one species and a different apomorphy with another. Cladistics looks for the simplest explanation when trying to decide between different results of analysis. Using the simplest explanation in cladistics is called parsimony. A German entomologist named Willi Hennig (1913–1976) was the first to popularize the use of cladistic analysis. In his writings, Hennig called an ancestor species and its entire descendant species a clade. Eventually, Hennig's methods of looking

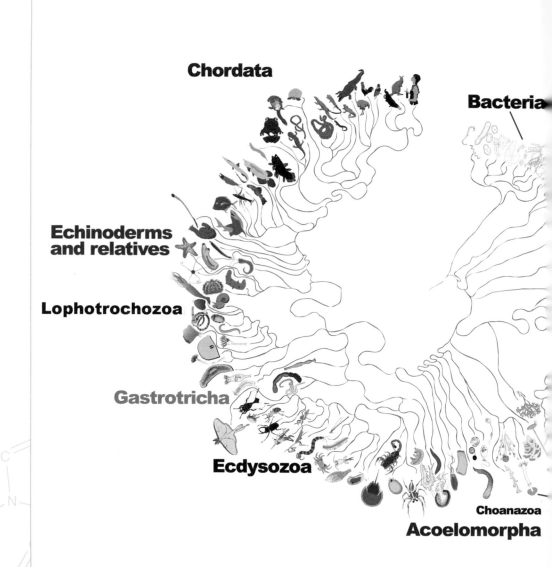

Chordata

Bacteria

Echinoderms
and relatives

Lophotrochozoa

Gastrotricha

Ecdysozoa

Choanazoa

Acoelomorpha

This cladogram shows the tree of life. All organisms are related to one another. Bacteria are distantly related to humans and other chordates.

Archaea

Amitochondriate "Excavates"

Discricristales

Chromalveolates

Radiolarians and relatives

Plantae

Amoebozoa

Fungi

for evolutionary relationships became known as cladistics.

Hennig was not the first person to suggest using the methods he described, but he was the first person to give clear rules for using cladistics. Hennig said that cladistics should only be used to infer relationships between the species being analyzed. For example, a cladogram was created using characters of different cat species, such as domestic cats, leopards, and lions. The cladogram could only be used to see how those cat species might be related. According to Hennig, the cat species cladogram could not be used to guess how the different cat species are related to domestic dogs because dogs were not included in the analysis.

Hennig also suggested that only synapomorphies could be used to decide which species are most closely related to one another. Synapomorphies are apomorphies that are shared between species. Remember that an apomorphy is a new trait that is different from the trait of a common ancestor. Cladists theorize that if a new form of a trait is found in two different species, it is more likely that they inherited the new trait from the same ancestor than adapted to develop the same trait twice.

Cladograms represent nested phylogenies. Nested simply means that the bigger group of the clade is subdivided into smaller groups of related sister groups. Sister groups are two groups that branch off from each other on the cladogram.

A cladogram that shows the order in which different related species branched off from each other is called a rooted cladogram. A cladogram that shows relationships with no chronological order is said to be unrooted.

Disagreements Caused by Cladistics

Cladistics sometimes clashes with the classification system developed by traditional taxonomists. For example, for a long time all snakes, lizards, crocodiles, and other scaly land animals have belonged in a class called Reptilia. Robins, blue jays, and pink flamingos belong to a class called Aves. Dogs, bears, and people belong to a class called Mammalia. Cladists disagree with this way of classification. If representative species from each group were analyzed on a rooted cladogram, the cladogram would show that all three groups shared a common ancestor. A saltwater crocodile, however,

Hennig's Phylogenetic Systematics

Willi Hennig called his method of cladistic analysis phylogenetic systematics. He never actually used the term "cladistics" in his writings, which focused on the relationships among the larvae of Diptera (the order of insects that includes flies, mosquitoes, and gnats). The word "cladistic" was first used by other zoologists working in the 1960s.

would be evolutionarily closer to this common ancestor than a pink flamingo because the crocodile and the common ancestor share lots of characteristics. A German shepherd, which shares the fewest common characteristics, would be evolutionarily the furthest away from the common ancestor.

Humans are often classified in their own family, called Hominidae. Other primates, such as chimpanzees, apes, and spider monkeys, are placed in an entirely different family, called Pongidae. If scientists create a cladogram by analyzing DNA sections, they see that chimpanzees and humans are more closely related than chimpanzees and spider monkeys. Primatologists, taxonomists, and cladists are still debating how the primate order should be divided to reflect true relationships.

Cladistics is an attractive way to look at phylogenetic relationships, but even cladistics can produce debatable and confusing results.

CHAPTER five

The Ever-Changing Science of Classification

For more than two thousand years, scientists classified living creatures into two groups called plants and animals. Plants are green and grow from the ground. Animals are often visible, noisy, and usually motile, meaning they can move about. The differences seemed clear enough. Since the 1600s and the invention of microscopes, scientists have learned even more about the difference between animals and plants. Plant cells have a thick wall around them. A thin membrane with no thick cell wall surrounds the cells of animals. Scientists called these large groups kingdoms and the idea of kingdoms is still very important. But the science of classification has changed a great deal over time.

The microscopic animalcules that Dutch naturalist Antoni van Leeuwenhoek (1632–1723) had discovered, some in his own bodily waste, were very simple creatures. Still, some photosynthesized, like plants, and some swam around, powered by tiny tails called

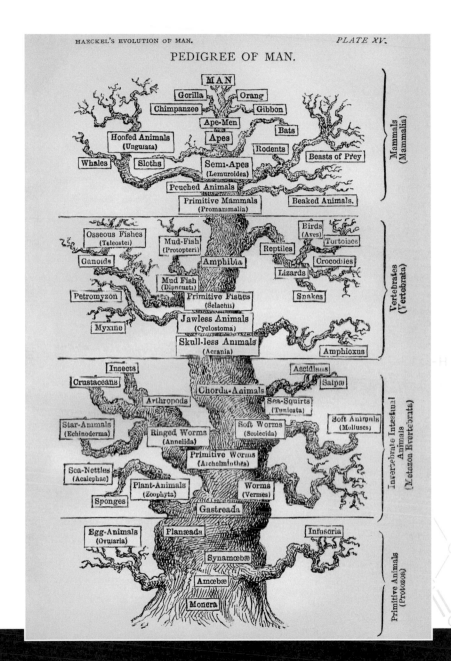

Ernest Haeckel agreed with Charles Darwin that all organisms were related through evolutionary relationships. He drew this sketch of the tree of life in 1879, which shows that he believed humans to be the most evolved of all creatures.

flagella. Scientists used these observations to classify them as plants or animals. Other microscopic organisms, however, foiled scientists' efforts to classify them. The euglena, a single-celled creature discovered by Leeuwenhoek, was motile and had a primitive eye-spot. But it also had the ability to photosynthesize.

The Addition of Kingdoms

In 1866, a German scientist named Ernst Haeckel suggested a third kingdom, called Protista. Haeckel was a firm believer in Darwin's theory of evolution. He believed that very similar organisms, such as dogs and wolves, came from a common ancestor relatively recently. He reasoned that very different organisms, like dogs and houseflies, had a common ancestor much longer ago. The common ancestor of dogs and common bacteria would have existed even longer ago still. Haeckel hypothesized

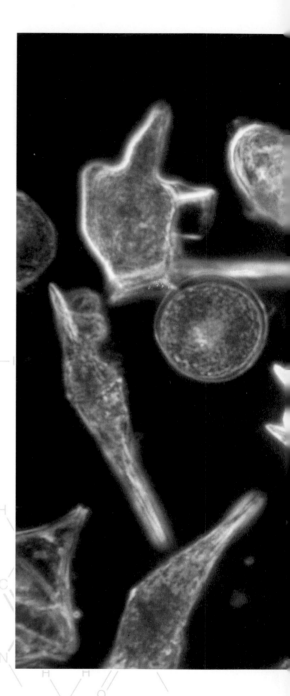

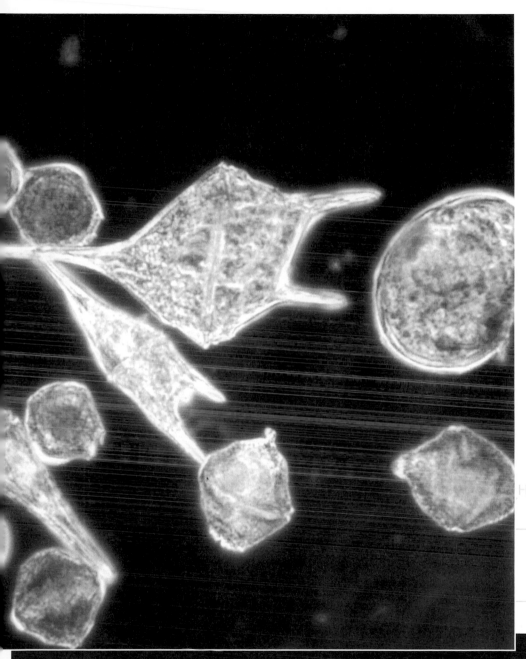

Dinoflagellates are eukaryotes in the kingdom Protoctista. Like animals, dinoflagellates can move, and their cells have organelles and a nucleus. Some dinoflagellates can also photosynthesize energy just like plants.

that these new microscopic organisms that Leeuwenhoek had described might be the common ancestor of all plants and animals. These microorganisms were so small, so simple, and so completely different from other animals and plants that they could be the most ancient common ancestors of all life.

Haeckel noticed that the microorganisms were similar to both plants and animals in some ways. If these creatures were the common ancestors of all organisms, he pointed out, then they could not be called a plant or an animal. So Haeckel suggested that these tiny living creatures should be placed into their own kingdom.

Haeckel's creation of a third kingdom based on how creatures were related signaled a tremendous change in classification. Not only were people used to just two kingdoms, but until Haeckel's time, scientists grouped life based on an organism's appearance or behavior. Tigers, lions, and cheetahs all have a furry, slinky appearance and are carnivorous, meaning that they eat other animals. They are easily grouped as animals, particularly as cats. Fir trees, hemlock trees, and blue spruce trees all have needles and cones. They are easily classified as pines: soft, woody plants. These living organisms are easily grouped by their appearance and behavior.

Darwin's theory of evolution by natural selection showed that life began with very simple organisms and changed over a very long time. Haeckel used this idea of a progression to group creatures according to how they were related.

Microscopes became more powerful through the early part of the twentieth century. Scientists continued to study microorganisms and began to realize just how different all these protists were from each other. Perhaps they should not all be in the same kingdom.

In 1956, a scientist named Herbert Copeland tried to solve this problem by splitting Haeckel's kingdom Protista into two groups. He put the prokaryotes, which had no nucleus, in a new kingdom he called Mychota. He put the eukaryotes, with their complex cell structure, many of them multicellular, in a group he called Protoctista. This group contained red algae, dinoflagellates, fungi, and the single-celled creatures that had a nucleus.

Copeland was just one of a large group of scientists who realized that having a nucleus and complex cell structure was an enormous step in evolution. Bacteria clearly were very simple. They had only a cell wall, cytoplasm, which is everything contained within the plasma membrane cell, and sometimes one or more whiplike structures, called flagella, that served to move them around. Bacteria have fewer specialized structures within the cell, only photosynthetic membrane systems and gas vesicles.

Eukaryotes had a nucleus that held their DNA. The cells of eukaryotes also had special structures to help make food, digest food, manufacture proteins, and many other things. Scientists saw that these structures function like the organs in an animal and called them organelles.

It was not long before scientists saw that another group of organisms was different enough to deserve its own kingdom. In the past fungi had been included in the plant kingdom or, in Copeland's system, Protoctista. Like plants, fungi grow out of the ground or on other materials and they do not move around as animals do.

In 1959, American biologist Robert H. Whittaker (1920–1980) proposed that fungi are very different from plants and should have their own kingdom. Whittaker studied the ecology of fungi. He pointed out that fungi hold a very different place in the food chain. Plants are called producers. They use chlorophyll to trap the energy of sunlight and produce sugar. Trees, bushes, and grasses all use broad green leaves to capture the energy of sunlight, produce food, and grow. Plants are then eaten by many other life-forms. Nearly all of Earth's energy comes from the sun and forms the base of the food chain.

Fungi hold a completely different place on the food chain. Fungi break down, or digest, other organisms for their food. Most people first experience fungi on rotting food. When food goes bad or gets moldy, it is usually a fungus growing on the food, digesting it. The mold absorbs the nutrients and uses them for energy it needs to live and grow. Fungi are known as nature's recyclers. Anything that dies is used as food by fungi. It happens with an animal carcass in the forest or by the side of the road. It happens when bread, grapes, or cheese are kept in the house too long.

By recognizing Fungi as a separate kingdom, Whittaker suggested that there were five kingdoms: Plantae, Animalia, Monera, Protista, and Fungi. Whittaker's five kingdoms arrangement quickly became accepted. This system of five kingdoms is still taught in many schools today. Changes to the tree of life did not stop, however.

Another Tool for the Classification of Living Organisms

Just as the invention of the microscope led to new discoveries, new technologies again played a role in a major advance. By the early 1970s, scientists could sequence, or read the order of, DNA and RNA. These genetic molecules make up the instructions that an organism uses to live, grow, and reproduce. Parts of the DNA are called genes. Some of these genes can be found in all organisms. These genes change bit by bit as populations evolve. Close relatives, like humans and chimpanzees, are very similar genetically. The more distant relatives, such as humans and slime mold, are much less similar genetically.

In the early 1970s, Carl R. Woese, an American molecular biologist, was studying bacterial RNA. Woese and his team compared one particular gene found in a mouse, in duckweed, in yeast, and in a few species of bacteria. The results proved to be historic.

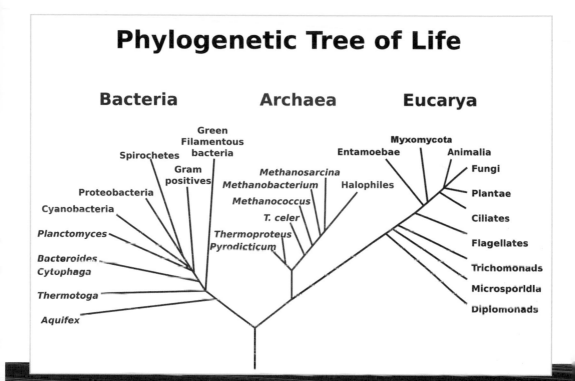

A phylogenetic tree of living organisms shows the domains Bacteria, Archaea, and Eukarya (sometimes spelled "Eucarya"). The domains were discovered when a scientist named Carl Woese compared the RNA of different types of bacteria and other organisms.

Woese and his team confirmed that the mouse, the duckweed, and the yeast were closely related—surprisingly close, considering how different the organisms look to the naked eye. The real surprise, however, came when Woese examined the relationships between the various bacteria. Two of the species of bacteria, called methanogens because they produce methane, showed that they were very distant relatives of the other two species of bacteria. In fact, the methane producers were so distantly related to the other bacteria that they were actually closer relatives to the mouse, the

Extremophiles and Their Amazing Living Conditions

Many archaea and some bacteria live under extreme living conditions and so are called extremophiles. For many years, it was thought that boiling water and cooking food killed all microorganisms and kept people's food safe. Cooking is important to the safety of food. Members of the domain Archaea, however, have been found living in the hot springs of Yellowstone National Park where water temperatures average near boiling! Even in the geysers of Yellowstone, small organisms have been found. These organisms, called hyperthermophiles,

Scientists have discovered giant tube worms, bacteria, and other organisms living in the extreme environments near thermal vents in the ocean floor.

are not just able to survive in these temperatures, they actually flourish. Scientists have seen that in many cases, these prokaryotes reproduce faster as the temperature increases.

Some extremophiles have also been found living near black smokers at the bottom of the Pacific Ocean, at depths of 7,000 feet (2,134 m). A black smoker is a vent, or hole, from which superheated mineral-rich water rises from deep within Earth's crust. One such extremophile is a type of bacteria that lives within the giant tube worms that grow near these smokers. This bacteria lives symbiotically with the giant tube worm in waters that reach temperatures of 750°F (399°C)! That is well above the boiling point of water, which under standard conditions at sea level is roughly 212°F (100°C). The water does not boil because the weight of the ocean's water at these depths keeps it in a liquid state.

Another type of extremophile, called an acidophile, thrives in superacidic sulfur-rich fields that form near some active volcanoes in Japan and Italy. The soil there has a pH of zero.

The ability of these life-forms to withstand such extraordinary conditions has led some scientists to speculate that these forms of life may have been carried to Earth from other planets by meteorites. Scientists also hypothesize that life may exist on Mars or even Jupiter's moon Europa. These amazing discoveries led scientists to look closer at the planet Earth in hopes of making an amazing discovery about life on other worlds.

duckweed, and the yeast. It was almost as if they should be in their own kingdom.

Woese decided to divide the different types of bacteria into two groups, called Archaea and Bacteria. But he did not make these groups kingdoms. The two groups were such distant relatives that Woese created a whole new rank above kingdom, called domain.

The domain Bacteria contains many single-celled organisms that people have experience with. The Bacteria species *Escherichia coli*, popularly known as *E. coli*, lives in people's bodies and helps digestion but sometimes makes them sick. The species *Mycobacterium tuberculosis* causes the deadly disease tuberculosis that kills about two million people annually.

The domain Archaea is also made up of single-celled organisms. The members of Archaea differ from those of Bacteria in the proteins within their genetic material. They are found throughout the world, in the oceans as well as in unusual environments, such as hot springs. Many eat strange foods, like ammonia or metal ions, instead of using sunlight for energy.

The third domain, Eukarya, is the domain of eukaryotic organisms, which means they have complex cells with a nucleus. This domain includes plants, animals, and fungi as well as protists. All the kingdoms that were once thought to exist are only a small part of the living world. The species of Archaea and Bacteria easily outweigh all the animals, plants, and fungi on this planet!

This shift in focus from eukaryotes to prokaryotes represented a historic change. For most of history, life as people knew it was fairly "advanced": humans, birds, rose bushes, oak trees. Even a simple animal, such as a jellyfish, or a simple plant, such as moss, is multicellular. All these organisms are eukaryotes. With the invention of microscopes, the use of Darwin's theory of evolution, and the application of nucleic acid sequencing techniques, it slowly became clear that the majority of life on Earth was prokaryotic.

This Pacific yew tree in Washington State is part of a genetics research project conducted by the U.S. Forest Service.

Always a Hypothesis

Science is always changing. The names and classifications of organisms are based on relationships to other organisms and people are never absolutely certain what those relationships are. Scientists try their best to figure out the relationships using fossils, DNA, and other methods, but they will always find new evidence. With the new evidence, there will be new ways to classify organisms. So the system of classification will always be changing and the tree of life will never be truly complete.

In the past, the best systems of classification classified animals and plants as the only organisms. Fungi used to be included in the plant kingdom. It is now known that fungi are more closely related to animals! Scientists also know that plants, animals, and fungi are only a tiny fraction of all life on Earth. A small handful of soil may contain as many different kinds of prokaryotes as there are species of mammals on Earth. There are also an estimated half million or more species of Archaea and Bacteria that remain undiscovered. There is so much left to find.

The Importance of Classification of Living Organisms

It has always been the dream of people to learn about the natural world and to name and classify all the new creatures and organisms that are discovered. There are other reasons, however, that accurate classification of organisms is important.

Humans still use many species of plants, fungi, and bacteria for medicine, for improving farming techniques, and to manufacture foods, such as bread, wine, and cheese. The lowly yew bush, a common shrub in the United States, has a chemical in its needles that helps to fight breast cancer. Some types of the yew produce the chemical more effectively than others. And closely related shrubs may even synthesize other cancer-fighting chemicals. Knowing the relationship between various yew bushes may help researchers find new drugs for treatment.

The expanding human population is changing the planet. Humans are working to prevent those changes from making living things go extinct. Species such as the giant panda, the jaguar, the gray wolf, the Atlantic salmon, and the Pitcher's thistle are in danger of going extinct. Knowing what their closest relatives are may help scientists find creatures that these threatened species can breed with. This will increase their chance of survival.

The classification of living organisms will be forever changing just as it was more than five thousand years ago. Classification will always be important for healing, living, eating, and preserving life on Earth.

Glossary

apomorphy A trait that is unique to an ancestral species and all descendants.

cladistics The classification of organisms into an evolutionary tree based solely on shared synapomorphies.

class The category in the Linnaean system of classification just below phylum.

conserved characteristic A trait that does not disappear quickly as a species evolves; this is useful in finding relationships between organisms.

domain The highest taxonomic rank. There are three domains: Archaea, Bacteria, and Eukarya.

dorsal nerve chord A hollow chord that runs dorsal to the notochord. It is present for part of the life cycle in all of the phylum Chordata.

eukaryote An organism whose cell or cells contain nuclei and other complex structures with membranes.

family The category in the Linnaean system of classification just below order.

genus The category in the Linnaean system of classification just below family; it is a mandatory part of a species name.

homology Any trait shared between organisms that is due to shared ancestry.

homoplasies Similar traits formed by convergence.

infer To reach a conclusion after having made a series of observations.

kingdom Highest category in the Linnaean system of classification; there were originally two kingdoms: plants and animals. One current system recognizes six.

microorganism An organism that is invisible to the naked eye, thus microscopic, and usually single-celled.

morphology The structure and form of an organism; it is often used to classify the organism.

notochord A flexible support structure to which muscles may attach. It is present for part of the life cycle in all of the phylum Chordata.

order The category in the Linnaean system of classification just below class.

parsimony The assumption that traits of an organism are unlikely to evolve twice and so are more likely to be synapomorphies.

pharyngeal slits Perforations in the pharynx wall that are used to filter food; these are present for part of the life cycle in all of the phyla Chordata and Hemichordata.

phenetics Classification based on similarities in physical characteristics.

phylogenetics Using evolutionary relationships to classify organisms.

phylum The category in the Linnaean system of classification just below kingdom.

prokaryote A single-celled microorganism classified as Archaea or Bacteria that has a very simple cell structure and no nuclei or other membrane-bound organelles.

species A name that differentiates the organism from all others in the genus; it is part of Aristotle's naming system. Every species is identified by a binomial consisting of its genus and species.

symbiotic An interactive relationship in which two species live closely together, usually to the advantage of both.

synapomorphy A trait shared among groups that came from their common ancestor.

systematics The study of the diversity of life and the relationships between organisms.

taxon A group of organisms within a formal nomenclature.

taxonomy The science of classifying living organisms.

vesicle An air- or fluid-filled sac.

For More Information

American Museum of Natural History
Central Park West at 79th Street
New York, NY 10024-5192
(212) 769-5100
Web site: http://www.amnh.org
The museum researches and interprets its collections and helps teach the
   public about various cultures and the natural world.

American Society of Plant Taxonomists
Department of Botany 3165
Laramie, WY 82071
(307) 766-2556
Web site: http://www.aspt.net
This group promotes the research and teaching of taxonomy, systematics,
   and phylogeny of plants.

Linnean Society of London
Burlington House
Piccadilly, London W1J 0BF
England
+44 (0)20 7434 4479
Web site: http://linnean.org/index.php?id=1
The Linnean Society of London was founded in 1788 and is the world's
   oldest active biological society. The organization works to cultivate the
   science of natural history.

National Museum of Natural History
Smithsonian Institution
P.O. Box 37012

Washington, DC 20013-7012
Web site: http://www.mnh.si.edu
The National Museum of Natural History provides research, exhibitions,
    collections, and education programs on natural science.

National Science Foundation
4201 Wilson Boulevard
Arlington, VA 22230
(703) 292-5111
Web site: http://www.nsf.gov
This agency was formed by the U.S. government "to promote the progress
    of science; to advance the national health, prosperity, and welfare; to
    secure the national defense."

UNESCO
7 Place de Fontenoy
75352 Paris 075P
France
+33 (0)1 45 68 10 00
Web site: http://portal.unesco.org
UNESCO promotes international cooperation in the sciences and carries
    out freshwater, marine, ecological, and earth science programs.

U.S. Fish and Wildlife Service
Division of Information Resources and Technology Management
4401 North Fairfax Drive, Suite 340
Arlington, VA 22203
(703) 358-1729
Web site: http://www.fws.gov
A bureau within the Department of the Interior, the U.S. Fish and Wildlife
    Service works to preserve, protect, and help the habitats of fish,
    wildlife, and plants.

Willi Hennig Society
Invertebrate Zoology
American Museum of Natural History
Central Park West at 79th Street
New York, NY 10024
(212) 769-5638
Web site: http://www.cladistics.org
The Willi Hennig Society promotes the field of phylogenetic systematics.

Web Sites

Due to the changing nature of Internet links, Rosen Publishing has developed
an online list of Web sites related to the subject of this book. This site is
updated regularly. Please use this link to access the list:

http://www.rosenlinks.com/gen/class

For Further Reading

Anderson, Bridget. *The Kingdoms of Life: Classification* (World Science: Come Learn with Me). West Palm Beach, FL: Lickle Publishing, 2003.

Angier, Natalie. *The Canon: A Whirligig Tour of the Beautiful Basics of Science*. New York, NY: Mariner, 2008.

Claybourne, Anna. *Can You Tell a Skink from a Salamander?* Chicago, IL: Heinemann-Raintree, 2005.

Dunn, Rob. *Every Living Thing: Man's Obsessive Quest to Catalog Life, from Nanobacteria to New Monkeys*. New York, NY: HarperCollins, 2009.

Freedman, Jeri. *The Applications and Limitations of Taxonomy (in Classification of Organisms): An Anthropology of Current Thought* (Contemporary Discourse in the Field of Biology). New York, NY: Rosen Publishing Group, 2005.

Fullick, Anne. *Variation and Classification* (Life Science in Depth). Chicago, IL: Heinemann-Raintree, 2006.

Gibson, J. Phil. *Natural Selection* (Science Foundations). New York, NY: Chelsea House Publications, 2009.

Lennox, James. "Aristotle's Biology." *Stanford Encyclopedia of Philosophy* (Fall 2008 Edition). Retrieved June 10, 2009 (http://plato.stanford.edu/archives/fall2008/entries/aristotle-biology).

National Geographic. "A Passion for Order." Retrieved August 30, 2009 (http://ngm.nationalgeographic.com/print/2007/06/linnaeus-name-giver/david-quammen-text).

Pobst, Sandra. *National Geographic Investigates: Animals on the Edge: Science Races to Save Species Threatened with Extinction*. Des Moines, IA: National Geographic Children's Books, 2008.

Rose, Elizabeth. *Classification of Living and Nonliving Things* (The Life Science Library). New York, NY: PowerKids Press, 2006.

Schultz, Mark, Zander Cannon, and Kevin Cannon. *The Stuff of Life: A Graphic Guide to Genetics and DNA*. New York, NY: Hill and Wang, 2009.

Simpson, Kathleen. *National Geographic Investigates: Genetics: From DNA to Designer Dogs*. Des Moines, IA: National Geographic Children's Books, 2008.

Simpson, Michael. *Plant Systematics*. New York, NY: Academic Press, 2005.

Solway, Andrew. *Classifying Mammals* (Classifying Living Things). Chicago, IL: Heinemann Library, 2003.

Stewart, Melissa. *Classification of Life*. Minneapolis, MN. Twenty-First Century Books, 2008.

Strauss, Rachel. *Tree of Life: The Incredible Biodiversity of Life on Earth*. Tonawanda, NY: Kids Can Press, 2004.

Windows to the Universe. "Classification of Living Things." Retrieved July 20, 2009 (http://www.windows.ucar.edu/tour/link=/earth/Life/classification_intro.html&edu=high).

Winston, Robert. *Evolution Revolution*. New York, NY: DK Publishing, 2009.

Wood, A. J., and Clint Twist. *Charles Darwin and the Beagle Adventure*. Somerville, MA: Templar Books, 2009.

Zabludoff, Marc. *The Protoctist Kingdom*. Tarrytown, NY: Marshall Cavendish Benchmark, 2006.

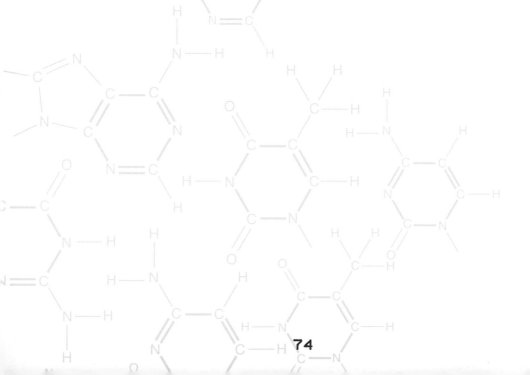

Bibliography

American Cetacean Society. "Right Whale." Retrieved August 30, 2009 (http://www.acsonline.org/factpack/RightWhale.htm).

Blunt, Wilfrid. *The Compleat Naturalist: A Life of Linnaeus.* New York, NY: Viking Press, 1971.

Busch Gardens. "Animals: Mammals." Retrieved August 15, 2009 (http://www.seaworld.org/animal-info/Animal-bytes/animalia/eumetazoa/coelomates/deuterostomes/chordata/craniata/mammalia/index.htm).

Montana State University. "Butterflies and Moths of North America." Retrieved August 16, 2009 (http://www.butterfliesandmoths.org/species?l=1892).

National Aquarium in Baltimore. "Dolphins." Retrieved August 18, 2009 (http://www.aqua.org/downloads/pdf/Dolphins.pdf).

National Center for Biotechnology Information. "Systematics and Molecular Phylogenetics." Retrieved August 10, 2009 (http://www.ncbi.nlm.nih.gov/About/primer/phylo.html).

National Geographic. "Right Whale." Retrieved August 20, 2009 (http://animals.nationalgeographic.com/animals/mammals/right-whale.html).

National Geographic. "Whale Shark Profile." Retrieved August 20, 2009 (http://animals.nationalgeographic.com/animals/fish/whale-shark.html).

Parker, Sybil, ed. *Synopsis and Classification of Living Things.* New York, NY: McGraw-Hill, 1982.

Penguin World. "Aptenodytes." Retrieved August 10, 2009 (http://www.penguinworld.com/types/aptenodytes.html).

Rose, Kenneth Jon. *Classification of the Animal Kingdom: An Introduction to Evolution.* New York, NY: D. McKay Co., 1980.

Rose, Michael, R. *Darwin's Spectre.* 1st ed. Princeton, NJ: Princeton University Press, 1998.

Simpson, George Gaylord. *Principles of Animal Taxonomy.* New York, NY: Columbia University Press, 1990.

Stace, Clive Anthony. *Plant Taxonomy and Biosystematics.* 2nd ed. New York, NY: Cambridge University Press, 1992.

Stearn, William T. *Botanical Latin.* 4th ed. Portland, OR: Timber Press, 2004.

Tobin, Kate. "Extremophile Hunter." Science Nation. Retrieved August 8, 2009 (http://www.nsf.gov/news/special_reports/science_nation/extremophile.jsp).

University of California Museum of Paleontology. "Understanding Evolution." Retrieved August 5, 2009 (http://evolution.berkeley.edu/evolibrary/home.php).

University of Virginia. "Phylogenetic Systematics." Retrieved August 4, 2009 (http://www.faculty.virginia.edu/evolutionlabs/Phylogenetics_Page.html).

Willi Hennig Society. "Willi Hennig." Retrieved August 4, 2009 (http://www.cladistics.org/about/hennig.html).

Wilson, Edward O. *The Diversity of Life.* Cambridge, MA: Belknap Press of Harvard University Press, 1992.

Index

A

Acacia, 32
acidophiles, 63
Agaporomorphus colberti, 32
Animalia, 28, 60
apomorphies, 47, 49, 51
Aptenodytes, 28
Archaea, 62, 64, 66
Aristotle, 6, 8, 10, 11, 13, 14, 15,
   16, 23, 25
Arthropoda, 28
Aves, 28, 52

B

Bacteria, 64, 66
Bauhin, Gaspard, 18, 22
Bauhin, Jean, 18, 22
Beagle, HMS, 35, 37
binomial nomenclature, 22, 23, 33

C

Cesalpino, Andrea, 16, 18
Cetacea, 43
Chondrichthyes, 43
Chordata, 28
cladograms, 48, 49, 51, 52, 53
classification
  cladistics and, 47–53
  early systems, 6–15
  ever-changing, 54–67
  modern systems, 16–33
  phylogenetics and, 34–46, 47
Colbert, Stephen, 32
conserved traits, 45–46, 47
convergence, 40, 41, 42–43
Copeland, Herbert, 58–59

D

Danaus, 28, 30
Darwin, Charles, 34–41, 46, 56,
   58, 64
derived traits, 47
dichotomus key, 26
Diptera, 52
divergence, 40
DNA, 46, 48, 49, 53, 59, 60, 66
duck-billed platypus, 30, 32

E

Ebers Papyrus, 6
E. coli, 64
embryology, 30
euglena, 56
Eukarya, 64
eukaryotes, 59, 64
extremophiles, 62–63

F

Fitzroy, Robert, 35
fossils, 18, 20, 66
fungi, 59–60, 64, 66

77

About the Author

Mark J. Lewis is an ecologist, science education content developer, and children's writer with five years of teaching experience in high school science and math in alternative education programs. He has studied the link between the loss of genetic diversity among the Pennsylvania forest understory and invasive species.

Photo Credits

Cover (top) Spencer Platt/Getty Images; cover (bottom), back cover, and interior © www.istockphoto.com/Gregory Spencer; p. 5 Tim Boyle/Getty Images; p. 7 The Bridgeman Art Library/Getty Images; pp. 8–9 Stephen Frink/Photographer's Choice/Getty Images; pp. 10–11 David B. Fleetham/Photolibrary/Getty Images; p. 12 Private Collection/The Bridgeman Art Library; p. 14 © www.istockphoto.com/niknikon; p. 17 Vanni/Art Resource, NY; p. 19 Buyenlarge/Getty Images; p. 21 Wikimedia Commons; p. 27 (top) © www.istockphoto.com/Scott Slattery; p. 27 (bottom) © www.istockphoto.com/Jan Will; p. 29 (top) © www.istockphoto.com/Doctor_bass; p. 29 (bottom) © www.istockphoto.com/George Clerk; p. 31 Kelly Miller and Quentin Wheeler; pp. 36–37 Down House/The Bridgeman Art Library; pp. 38–39 HIP/Art Resource, NY; p. 41 © Universal Images Group Limited/Alamy; p. 42 © www.istockphoto.com/Arvydas Kniuksta; p. 43 Shutterstock.com; pp. 44, 45 © www.istockphoto.com/Eric Isselée; pp. 48–49 Private Collection/Archives Charmet/The Bridgeman Art Library; pp. 50–51 © Nemo Ramjet/Photo Researchers, Inc.; p. 55 Wikimedia Commons; pp. 56–57 © Educational Images, Ltd./Custom Medical Stock Photography; p. 61 NASA/Wikimedia Commons; p. 62 © Nicolle Rager Fuller/National Science Foundation; p. 65 © Kevin Beebe/Custom Medical Stock Photo.

Designer: Nicole Russo; Editor: Kathy Kuhtz Campbell; Photo Researcher: Amy Feinberg